This book is for: _____

From: _____

On: _____

May the Bible light your way to
a closer friendship with God!

FRIENDS with GOD

DISCOVER

HOW to READ THE BIBLE

Written by Jeff White
Illustrated by David Harrington

Group | **lifetree**

Visit **MyLifetree.com** for more fun, faith-building stuff for kids!

Friends With God Discover How to Read the Bible

Copyright © 2019 Group Publishing, Inc./0000 0001 0362 4853
Lifetree™ is an imprint of Group Publishing, Inc.

Visit our website: **group.com**

Credits
Author: Jeff White
Illustrator: David Harrington
Chief Creative Officer: Joani Schultz
Senior Editors: Jan Kershner and Candace McMahan
Assistant Editor: Cherie Shifflett
Cover Design: Stephen Caine
Interior Design: Darrin Stoll

Scripture quotations are taken from the Holy Bible, New Living Translation, copyright © 1996, 2004, 2015 by Tyndale House Foundation. Used by permission of Tyndale House Publishers, Inc., Carol Stream, Illinois 60188. All rights reserved.

ISBN 978-1-4707-5504-1 (hardcover)
ISBN 978-1-4707-5503-4 (ePub)

10 9 8 7 6 5 4 3 2 1   28 27 26 25 24 23 22 21 20 19

Printed in China.
001 China 1018

TABLE OF CONTENTS

Let's Explore the Bible!

"Jesus used many similar stories and illustrations to teach the people as much as they could understand."

Mark 4:33

From "once upon a time" to "happily ever after," you know a good story when you read one. The Bible is the *ultimate* true story. It tells us what God has done from the beginning of time, what's going to happen at the end of the world, and some of the best stuff in between.

But what are all these stories for? And why should you read them? I'm here to tell you! God created the Bible to help *you* discover how much God loves you and wants to be with you as your forever friend. All the stories, poems, prophecies, and letters in the Bible give *you* the answers to life's questions and problems. So now *you* can grow closer to God no matter what you're going through. That's because I'm always with you. And the Bible can help you remember that.

How should you read the Bible? With an open heart and an open mind to understand just how much God loves you. Because God really, really, *really* loves you, my friend.

Your friend,
Jesus

The BIBLE
Is a Mini-Library

The Bible is a *giant* book. I mean it's *really* big. But it's also a collection of smaller books—66 in all.

You might think of it as God's library. Just like a library, this amazing collection of books is divided into sections. The first section is called the Old Testament. It includes everything that happened before Jesus was born. The second section is called the New Testament, and it includes everything that happened after Jesus was born.

The Old Testament has 39 books, which are grouped into four parts:

The first five books (also called the Pentateuch) tell us all about the laws God made for his people and why they needed them. It covers the story of Creation through the start of the nation of Israel. It explains why God created us and how much he loves us.

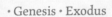

· Genesis · Exodus
· Leviticus · Numbers
· Deuteronomy

The next 12 books tell us the history of the Israelites, God's people, especially all the ups and downs of their friendship with God.

· Joshua · Judges · Ruth
· 1 & 2 Samuel · 1 & 2 Kings
· 1 & 2 Chronicles · Ezra
· Nehemiah · Esther

These books show us the powerful feelings people have about their friendship with God.

· Job · Psalms
· Proverbs
· Ecclesiastes
· Song of Solomon

God used many prophets— people who speak God's truth— to give messages to his people and explain what friendship with God really means.

· Isaiah · Jeremiah · Lamentations
· Ezekiel · Daniel · Hosea · Joel
· Amos · Obadiah · Jonah · Micah
· Nahum · Habakkuk · Zephaniah
· Haggai · Zechariah · Malachi

The New Testament has 27 books, which are grouped into four parts:

Each of these books is a letter (also called epistle) written to people about their Christian faith and their friendship with God.

"Gospel" means "good news," and the good news is that Jesus came to take away our sins (the wrong things we do) so we can be friends with God. These four books tell us all about Jesus' life, including his birth, miracles, friendships, teachings, death, and resurrection.

· Matthew · Mark · Luke · John

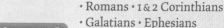

· Romans · 1 & 2 Corinthians
· Galatians · Ephesians
· Philippians · Colossians
· 1 & 2 Thessalonians
· 1 & 2 Timothy · Titus
· Philemon · Hebrews
· James · 1 & 2 Peter
· 1, 2, & 3 John · Jude

The New Testament gives us this one book all about the history of Jesus' first followers and the beginning of the Christian church.

· Acts

The New Testament has this one book of prophecy, which tells us how the world will end. Thankfully, everyone who believes in Jesus will live forever as friends with God!

· Revelation

"I will teach you hidden lessons from our past— stories we have heard and known, stories our ancestors handed down to us. We will not hide these truths from our children; we will tell the next generation about the glorious deeds of the Lord, about his power and his mighty wonders."

Psalm 78:2-4

11

CHAPTERS & VERSES

The Bible wasn't originally written with chapter and verse numbers. But the Bible is so big that people decided to mark it with numbers so it would be easy to find exactly what you're looking for.

With chapters and verses, it's super simple to find the Bible stories you want to read. Here's how to find one of the most popular verses in the Bible, John 3:16.

▸ First you find the book (John). Hint: It's in the New Testament.

▸ Then you find the third chapter in John.

▸ And then you find the 16th verse.
  (Look it up now. What does that verse say?)

"If you search for [God] with all your heart and soul, you will find him."

Deuteronomy 4:29

Jesus and Nicodemus

[23] Because of the miraculous signs Jesus did in Jerusalem at the Passover celebration, many began to trust in him. [24] But Jesus didn't trust them, because he knew all about people. [25] No one needed to tell him about human nature, for he knew what was in each person's heart.

[1] There was a man named Nicodemus, a Jewish religious leader, a Pharisee. [2] After dark one evening, he came to speak with Jesus. "Rabbi," he said, "we all know that God has sent you to teach us. Your miraculous signs are evidence that God is with you."

[3] Jesus replied, "I tell you the truth, unless you are born again,* you cannot see the Kingdom of God."

[4] "What do you mean?" exclaimed Nicodemus. "How can an old man go back into his mother's womb and be born again?"

[5] Jesus replied, "I assure you, no one can enter the Kingdom of God without being born of water and the Spirit.* [6] Humans can reproduce only human life, but the Holy Spirit gives birth to spiritual life.* [7] So don't be surprised when I say, 'You* must be born again.' [8] The wind blows wherever it wants. Just as you can hear the wind but can't tell where it comes from or where it is going, so you can't explain how people are born of the Spirit."

[9] "How are these things possible?" Nicodemus asked.

[10] Jesus replied, "You are a respected Jewish teacher, and yet you don't understand these things? [11] I assure you, we tell you what we know and have seen, and yet you won't believe our testimony. [12] But if you don't believe me when I tell you about earthly things, how can you possibly believe if I tell you about heavenly things? [13] No one has ever gone to heaven and returned. But the Son of Man* has come down from heaven. [14] And as Moses lifted up the bronze snake on a pole in the wilderness, so the Son of Man must be lifted up, [15] so that everyone who believes in him will have eternal life.*

[16] "For this is how God loved the world: He gave* his one and only Son, so that everyone who believes in him will not perish but have eternal life. [17] God sent his Son into the world not to judge the world, but to save the world through him.

[18] "There is no judgment against anyone who believes in him. But anyone who does not believe in him has already been judged for not believing in God's one and only Son. [19] And the judgment is based on this fact: God's light came into the world, but people loved the darkness more than the light, for their actions were evil. [20] All who do evil hate the light and refuse to go near it for fear their sins will be exposed. [21] But those who do what is right come to the light so others can see that they are doing what God wants.*"

John the Baptist Exalts Jesus

[22] Then Jesus and his disciples left Jerusalem and went into the Judean countryside. Jesus spent some time with them there, baptizing people.

[23] At this time John the Baptist was baptizing at Aenon, near Salim, because there was plenty of water there; and people kept coming to him for baptism. [24] (This was before John was thrown into prison.) [25] A debate broke out between John's disciples and a certain Jew* over ceremonial cleansing. [26] So John's disciples came to him and said, "Rabbi, the man you met on the other side of the Jordan River, the one you identified as the Messiah, is also baptizing people. And everybody is going to him instead of coming to us."

[27] John replied, "No one can receive anything unless God gives it from heaven. [28] You yourselves know how plainly I told you, 'I am not the Messiah. I am only here to prepare the way for him.' [29] It is the bridegroom who marries the bride, and the bridegroom's friend is simply glad to stand with him and hear his vows. Therefore, I am filled with joy at his success. [30] He must become greater and greater, and I must become less and less.

[31] "He has come from above and is greater than anyone else. We are of the earth, and we speak of earthly things, but he has come from heaven and is greater than anyone else.* [32] He testifies about what he has seen and heard, but how few believe what he tells them! [33] Anyone who accepts his testimony can affirm that God is true. [34] For he is sent by God. He speaks God's words, for God gives him the Spirit without limit. [35] The Father loves his Son and has put everything into his hands. [36] And anyone who believes in God's Son has eternal life. Anyone who doesn't obey

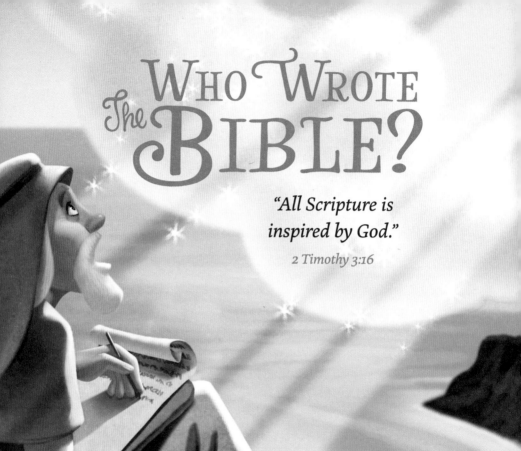

WHO WROTE The BIBLE?

"All Scripture is inspired by God."

2 Timothy 3:16

14

God didn't pick up a pen and write the Bible himself. Instead, God chose more than 40 people to write and tell his story. These people came from lots of different backgrounds; some were kings, some were fishermen or shepherds, others were businessmen or soldiers; one was even a doctor. They wrote with different writing styles, too. And some wrote about history, some wrote letters to friends, while others wrote poetry.

Here's the amazing thing about all these different writers: They were all inspired by God to write what they did. Some people say that the Bible is "God-breathed," which means that God spoke through these writers as they wrote.

Some of those writers were Moses, David, Daniel, Isaiah, and Paul. None of those men ever met each other, but they were all inspired to write a part of God's story.

And here's something else that's amazing. Even though these writers came from different cultures and different times in history, their writings agree with each other. They're all part of the same story, which is that God loves us and sent his Son, Jesus, to make it possible for us to become friends with God.

T·I·M·E·L·I·N·E
—OF—
The BIBLE

3000 B.C.—
Stonehenge is built in England

Abraham is born

1500 B.C.—
Coins are invented

God gives Moses the Ten Commandments

Creation

2500 B.C.—
Great Pyramid of Giza is built in Egypt

Jacob steals Esau's inheritance

Gideon defeats the Midianites

David
defeats
Goliath

Jonah is
swallowed by
a big fish

God saves
Daniel in the
lions' den

Jesus is
born!

Ruth and
Naomi travel
to Bethlehem

750 B.C.—
Fake teeth
are invented

Esther becomes
Xerxes' queen

God gives
Solomon
wisdom

200 B.C.—
Paper invented
in China

The events in the Bible took place thousands of years ago, but their truths remain as important and helpful as ever. Bible experts believe Moses wrote the first books of the Bible around 1400 B.C. (Before Christ), while the last books of the Bible were written in the years after Jesus' death.

Follow this timeline to see when key events in the Bible took place in history.

*"Through their faith, the people in days
of old earned a good reputation."*

Hebrews 11:2

FINDING JESUS
THROUGHOUT THE BIBLE

The whole Bible points to God's plan to bring us close to him through Jesus. In the Old Testament, we see God's people looking forward to a Messiah—a hero who will come and save them. In the New Testament, Jesus comes, and *he* is the Messiah—not just for the people of Israel, but for *everyone*.

You can find hints and clues about Jesus almost everywhere in the Old Testament. Here are a few examples:

In Genesis, God wanted to be with Adam and Eve, but their sin broke their relationship. But even back then, God had a plan to take away people's sins and bring us together with him again. That way is Jesus.

Read about Adam and Eve in Genesis 2–3.

In Exodus, the Jews celebrated the Passover to remember when God "passed over" their families and spared them from death. The Passover lamb was a sacrifice—a substitute for the people who would have died if God hadn't spared them. Jesus (who was also called the Lamb of God) gave his life as a sacrifice—a substitute—for the sins of all people.

Read about the Passover in Exodus 12.

"You search the Scriptures because you think they give you eternal life. But the Scriptures point to me!"

John 5:39

18

In 2 Samuel and 1 Chronicles, we read all about King David. David was Jesus' great-great-great-great-great- (plus about 20 more greats) grandfather. Before Jesus was born, God said the Messiah would come from David's family and that he would be born in Bethlehem, which is where David's great-grandma, Ruth, lived.

Read about God's promise to David in 2 Samuel 7 and 1 Chronicles 17.

Job had a lot of questions, and Jesus has all the answers. Job asked how he could approach God. (Jesus provides the way.) Job asked about life after death. (Jesus makes eternal life with God possible.) Job asked what's important in life. (Jesus tells us that believing in him is the most important thing.)

Read Jesus' answers in Matthew 5; 6; and 7.

Many of David's psalms tell us about things that would happen to Jesus. For example, Psalm 22 describes Jesus' death. Jesus even quoted from Psalm 22 when he was on the cross.

Read Psalm 22:1; then see what Jesus said in Matthew 27:46 and Mark 15:34.

Isaiah's prophecies about Jesus are amazing. Hundreds of years before they happened, Isaiah described Jesus' birth, his name, his ministry, his death, his resurrection, and how he'll come again to rule forever.

Read Isaiah 9:6-7 and Isaiah 53 to see prophecies about the coming of Jesus as the Messiah.

THE BIBLE By THE NUMBERS

PSALM 119 Psalms has the longest chapter of the Bible (Psalm 119) and the shortest (Psalm 117). **PSALM 117**

The shortest verse in the Bible is JOHN 11:35: "Then Jesus wept."

The stories of the Bible take place on **3** continents: Africa, Asia, and Europe.

Jesus fed **5,000** people with just **5** loaves of bread and **2** fish.

The Bible is the world's most-read book! According to Guinness World Records, more than **5** billion copies of the Bible have been printed.

40 You'll see the number **40** in several Bible stories:

* During Noah's flood, it rained **40** days and **40** nights.

* The Jews wandered in the wilderness for **40** years.

* David ruled as king for **40** years.

* Jesus fasted for **40** days in the wilderness.

* Jesus walked the earth for **40** days after his resurrection.

3 You can also find the number **3** a lot in the Bible:

* The Trinity is made of **3** persons: the Father, the Son, and the Holy Spirit.

* The Lord called Samuel **3** times.

* Jonah was in the belly of the fish for **3** days.

* Jesus came back to life after **3** days.

* Satan tempted Jesus **3** times.

* Peter denied Jesus **3** times.

2 books of the Bible are named after women: Ruth and Esther.

12 The number **12** often pops up in the Bible, too:

* Israel had **12** tribes.

* Jesus had **12** disciples.

* The disciples gathered **12** baskets of food after Jesus fed 5,000 people.

* In the New Jerusalem, the Tree of Life will produce **12** kinds of fruit.

HOW TO MARK YOUR BIBLE

If you have your own Bible, you can mark in it to help you understand and remember it better. This can also help you pay closer attention to what you're reading.

Here are some tips for how to mark your Bible:

▸ You can <u>underline</u> or highlight verses that have special meaning for you.

▸ You can circle or <u>underline</u> words that jump out at you. For example, you might underline the word *love* every time you see it.

▸ You can write short notes to remind yourself why a Bible verse has special meaning to you. AWESOME, that's SO cool!

▸ You can draw pictures or symbols in the margins (the empty spaces on the outer edge of the pages) to show how you feel about certain verses. ✿ ☺ !

▸ You might want to use certain colors to help you remember the kinds of verses you're reading. For example, you might use blue to underline prayers in the Bible, or you might use orange to underline God's promises.

▸ Colored pencils work well because they won't bleed through the paper, and you can erase them if you want to.

it all to you," he said, "if you will kneel down and worship me."

¹⁰"Get out of here, Satan," Jesus told him. "For the Scriptures say,

'You must worship the LORD your God
and serve only him.'*"

¹¹Then the devil went away, and angels came and took care of Jesus.

The Ministry of Jesus Begins

WOW!

¹²When Jesus heard that John had been arrested, he left Judea and returned to Galilee. ¹³He went first to Nazareth, then left there and moved to Capernaum, beside the Sea of Galilee, in the region of Zebulun and Naphtali. ¹⁴This fulfilled what God said through the prophet Isaiah:

¹⁵ "In the land of Zebulun and of Naphtali,
beside the sea, beyond the Jordan River,
in Galilee where so many Gentiles live,
¹⁶ the people who sat in darkness
have seen a great light.
And for those who lived in the land where
death casts its shadow,
a light has shined."*

¹⁷From then on Jesus began to preach, "Repent of your sins and turn to God, for the Kingdom of Heaven is near.*" ☺

The First Disciples

¹⁸One day as Jesus was walking along the shore of the Sea of Galilee, he saw two brothers—Simon, also called Peter, and Andrew—throwing a net into the water, for they fished for a living. ¹⁹Jesus called out to them, "Come, follow me, and I will show you how to fish for people!" ²⁰And they left their nets at once and followed him.

²¹A little farther up the shore he saw two other brothers, James and John, sitting in a boat with their father, Zebedee, repairing their nets. And he called them to come, too. ²²They immediately followed him, leaving the boat and their father behind.

Crowds Follow Jesus

²³Jesus traveled throughout the region of Galilee, teaching in the synagogues and announcing the Good News about the Kingdom. And he healed every kind of disease and illness. ²⁴News about him spread as far as Syria, and people soon began bringing to him all who were sick. And whatever their sickness or disease, or if they were demon possessed or epileptic or paralyzed—he healed them all. ²⁵Large crowds followed him wherever he went—people from Galilee, the Ten Towns,* Jerusalem, from all over Judea, and from east of the Jordan River.

The Sermon on the Mount

5 One day as he saw the crowds gathering, Jesus went up on the mountainside and sat down. His disciples gathered around him, ²and he began to teach them.

The Beatitudes

So cool!

³ "God blesses those who are poor and realize their need for him,*
for the Kingdom of Heaven is theirs.
⁴ God blesses those who mourn,
for they will be comforted.
⁵ God blesses those who are humble,
for they will inherit the whole earth.
⁶ God blesses those who hunger and thirst for justice,*
for they will be satisfied.
⁷ God blesses those who are merciful,
for they will be shown mercy.
⁸ God blesses those whose hearts are pure,
for they will see God.
⁹ God blesses those who work for peace,
for they will be called the children of God.
¹⁰ God blesses those who are persecuted for doing right,
for the Kingdom of Heaven is theirs.

¹¹"God blesses you when people mock you and persecute you and lie about you and say all sorts of evil things against you because you are my followers. ¹²Be happy about it! Be very glad! For a great reward awaits you in heaven. And remember, the ancient prophets were persecuted in the same way.

Teaching about Salt and Light

AWESOME!

¹³"You are the salt of the earth. But what good is salt if it has lost its flavor? Can you make it salty again? It will be thrown out and trampled underfoot as worthless.

WHAT *the* BIBLE IS

 The Bible *is* a love letter from God. God gave us the Bible because he loves us, and he wants us to understand *how much* he loves us. It's God speaking directly to us, telling us about the depths of his love.

 The Bible *is* God's story. From beginning to end, the Bible tells us how God started the world, all he's done to love his people, and what's in store for the people who love him back. It's the most epic story ever told.

 The Bible *is* all about relationship. Every story, every book, and every verse are about God's relationships with people—both individual people and communities of people. And a big purpose of the Bible is to help you love God and love other people.

WHAT *THE* BIBLE IS NOT

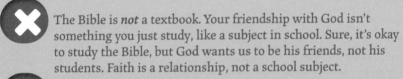

The Bible is *not* a textbook. Your friendship with God isn't something you just study, like a subject in school. Sure, it's okay to study the Bible, but God wants us to be his friends, not his students. Faith is a relationship, not a school subject.

The Bible is *not* a science book. The Bible shows us the wonders of God's creation in countless ways. But God didn't give us the Bible to answer scientific questions about the stars and planets or DNA. It's a book that tells us stories about people's relationships with God.

The Bible is *not* just a book of rules. Yes, it gives us a lot of very helpful advice and wisdom. But it's not just a handbook we pick up whenever we need instructions for doing something new. God's Word is so much more than that!

"People do not live by bread alone, but by every word that comes from the mouth of God."

Matthew 4:4

WHAT IS THAT?
OBJECTS IN THE BIBLE

As you read the Bible, you'll probably come across a lot of objects you've never heard of. Here are a few of them:

The Ark of the Covenant—In the book of Exodus and in other stories, you'll find this sacred box that contained the stone tablets with the Ten Commandments engraved on them. The box has two golden statues of angels across the top.

Shepherd's staff—Shepherds are popular characters in the Bible, and Jesus himself is called the Good Shepherd. Shepherds used these long, curved sticks, made out of wood, to help them reach and get hold of sheep that had gone astray.

Manna—God fed his people a food called manna while they were wandering in the wilderness. Every morning, the people would gather the manna off the ground, and it would be just enough to feed them for the whole day. The Bible says it tasted like honey cakes. God told Moses to save a jar of manna and put it in the Ark of the Covenant.

> *"The teaching of your word gives light,*
> *so even the simple can understand."*
>
> *Psalm 119:130*

 Idols—People sometimes worshipped idols instead of God. Idols were usually statues made of metal or wood, and they often had faces of people or animals. Today, anything that we love more than God could be called an idol.

 Armor—Soldiers almost always wore armor to protect themselves during battle. It was usually made of metal and thick leather. God says that when we believe in his truth, do the right things, and stay close to him, we have all the armor we need to protect us from harm.

 **Lamp**—We use electricity to turn on a lamp, but people in Bible times had to use lamps with oil and a flame to see at night. The lamp was a common symbol for God's Word, which can guide us through dark times.

MIRACLES OF THE BIBLE

God often used miracles to show his power and protect his people. The Bible records nearly 100 miracles in the Old and New Testaments. Here are some of the most amazing miracles—incredible, impossible things—in the Bible:

Creation—Creating the world and everything in it may be God's most amazing miracle of all. God spoke the words, and everything burst into being!

The 10 Plagues of Egypt—God sent 10 terrible plagues to show Pharaoh that God was powerful enough to set his people free.

Jesus Walks on Water—Jesus did the impossible to show his followers that they could do the impossible, too, when they had faith and relied on him.

> *"You are the God of great wonders! You demonstrate your awesome power among the nations."*
>
> *Psalm 77:14*

 Parting of the Red Sea—God, through Moses, split a sea in two so the Jews could walk to safety across dry ground.

 Fire From Heaven—To prove he is the one true God, God sent fire from heaven to burn up Elijah's offering.

 Saved From the Fire—When a king threw Shadrach, Meshach, and Abednego into a fiery furnace, the flames were so hot they killed the soldiers who tossed them in. But God kept his three faithful servants safe!

 Jesus Comes Back to Life—Three days after Jesus was killed, he came back to life to show that he held power over sin and death. He conquered death so you can live in heaven with God forever!

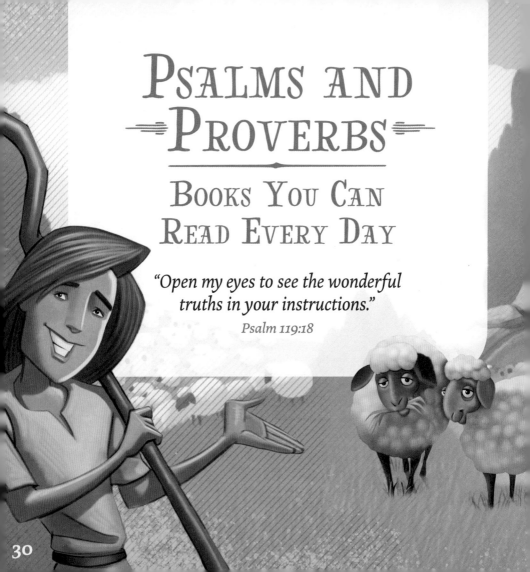

Psalms and Proverbs

Books You Can Read Every Day

"Open my eyes to see the wonderful truths in your instructions."

Psalm 119:18

The Bible is all about growing closer to God. Psalms and Proverbs are books of poetry that show how it feels to have a friendship with God.

Sometimes the writers were sad, sometimes they were scared, and sometimes they were as happy as happy could be. You can turn to Psalms and Proverbs every day, no matter how you're feeling, and they'll help you feel closer to God.

Here are some great places to start in Psalms and Proverbs:

- **What if you're worried and need help?** Read Psalm 121.
- **What if you need some extra protection in your life?** Read Psalm 91.
- **What if your life is so busy you can't think straight?** Read Psalm 46.
- **What if you don't know what to pray about?** Read Psalm 5.
- **What if you want to know more about Jesus?** Read Psalm 22.
- **What if you're confused about God?** Read Psalm 103.
- **What if your life feels out of control?** Read Psalm 23.
- **What if you want to feel close to God?** Read Psalm 117.
- **What if you need some advice about your future?** Read Proverbs 13.
- **What if you have a very short attention span?** Read any proverb.
- **What if you're having trouble choosing the right friends?** Read Proverbs 25.
- **What if you need wisdom?** Read Proverbs 3.

Did you know?
The book of Proverbs has 31 chapters. If you read one chapter each day, you could read the whole book in one month!

⇒ READ THE BIBLE ⇐
TO HEAR GOD
SPEAK TO YOU

"Your word is a lamp to guide my feet and a light for my path."

Psalm 119:105

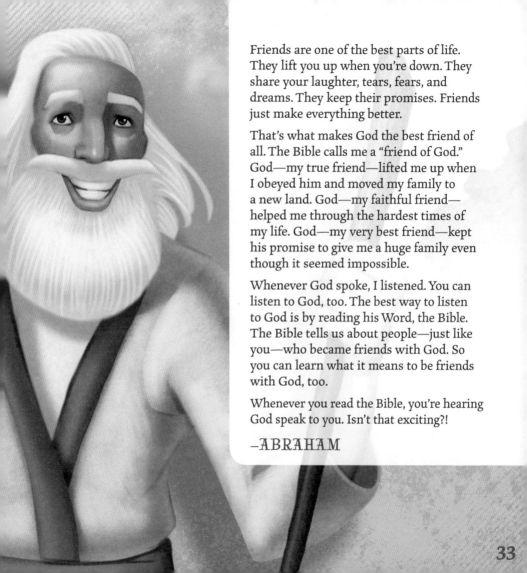

Friends are one of the best parts of life. They lift you up when you're down. They share your laughter, tears, fears, and dreams. They keep their promises. Friends just make everything better.

That's what makes God the best friend of all. The Bible calls me a "friend of God." God—my true friend—lifted me up when I obeyed him and moved my family to a new land. God—my faithful friend—helped me through the hardest times of my life. God—my very best friend—kept his promise to give me a huge family even though it seemed impossible.

Whenever God spoke, I listened. You can listen to God, too. The best way to listen to God is by reading his Word, the Bible. The Bible tells us about people—just like you—who became friends with God. So you can learn what it means to be friends with God, too.

Whenever you read the Bible, you're hearing God speak to you. Isn't that exciting?!

—ABRAHAM

33

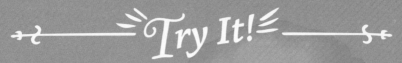

Try It!

Here's something you might not know. Psalm 117 is in the very middle of the Bible. Plus, it's the shortest chapter of the book of Psalms. Go ahead and read Psalm 117. What does this chapter mean to you? Write it below. Then read parts of the Bible before and after Psalm 117—no matter where you turn in the Bible, God has something to say to you.

Want to see how God spoke to people in the Bible?
Read these conversations God had with some of his friends.

- God gives instructions to Jacob—Genesis 35
- God gives Moses the Ten Commandments—Exodus 20
- God speaks to Solomon in a dream—1 Kings 3

READ THE BIBLE TO GROW CLOSER TO JESUS

"Come close to God, and God will come close to you."

James 4:8

I was just another girl in the crowd. As normal as normal could be. I laughed, cried, ate, slept, and stubbed my toes, just like you. There was nothing special about my life...until God chose me to do something no one else would ever do. God wanted me to be the mother of his Son—the Son of God!

Me?

To be honest, I was scared. When I got the news— from an angel, no less—I had a lump in my throat, a knot in the pit of my stomach, and a chill down my spine. Surely someone had made a mistake! But God doesn't make mistakes. God gave me a gift that I could share with the rest of the world...including you.

Because I'm not the only one God wanted to give Jesus to. Jesus may have been my baby, but he's also your best friend. God chose *you* to receive the gift of Jesus, too.

And that's not all. God has given you another precious gift: the Bible. The Bible is the story of Jesus—my son, God's Son—and how he came to bring you closer to God. Reading the Bible brings you closer to Jesus and knowing Jesus' heart.

There are so many amazing stories about Jesus in the Bible. I hope you'll read them all!

–MARY

Try It!

Read the Bible as if Jesus is sitting right next to you. Find two chairs. Sit in one and leave the other empty. Imagine Jesus sitting next to you as you read Matthew 19:13-14. Write about imagining Jesus sitting next to you.

Want to grow closer to Jesus?
Read these stories about some of the jaw-dropping things Jesus did.

▶ Jesus calms a storm—Mark 4:35-40

▶ Jesus walks on water—Matthew 14:22-33

▶ Jesus raises a man from the dead—John 11:1-44

⇒ READ THE BIBLE ⇐
❧ TO BE ❧
AMAZED BY GOD

"When I look at the night sky and see the work of your fingers—the moon and the stars you set in place—what are mere mortals that you should think about them, human beings that you should care for them?"

Psalm 8:3-4

God. Is. So. AMAZING!

God has done so many incredible things. For starters, God created the entire universe! He made the stars, the moon, oceans, forests, mountains, and everything in between. And God is so creative. He made every kind of colorful creature you could imagine—things with wings, stuff with fluff, and critters with glitter. (And *I* got to give them each a name.) I'm in awe!

The Bible is full of the most *astonishing* and *breathtaking* things. Making miracles and working wonders are God's specialty. But you know what the coolest part is? God's not done doing amazing things. When you become God's friend, you can be filled with God's Spirit, which is the most *powerful* and *extraordinary* thing of all. God's love can work through *you*.

And you know what else? God speaks to everyone—that means *you*—through his Word. So when you read the Bible, you're reading *exactly* what you need, exactly when you need it. How *amazing* is that?

—ADAM

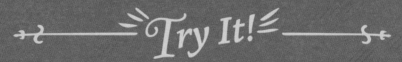

Try It!

Read the story of Creation in Genesis 2:4-23. As you read, imagine yourself in Adam's place—the first human God created—surrounded by so many new sounds, smells, and sights. Describe or draw what you think Eden looked like.

Want to be amazed by God?
Read these stories about God's power. Be prepared to be thunderstruck!

▸ God sends 10 plagues to Egypt—Exodus 7–12:33

▸ God makes the sun stand still—Joshua 10:12-14

▸ God raises Jesus from the dead—Matthew 28

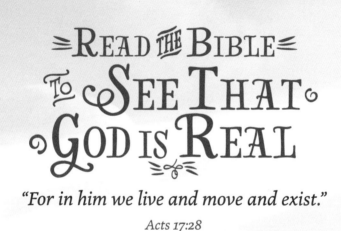

READ THE BIBLE TO SEE THAT GOD IS REAL

"For in him we live and move and exist."

Acts 17:28

I've seen God do some *amazing* things—jaw-dropping miracles that took my breath away. Like the time God sent fire down from the sky and turned a giant altar into a pile of smoking ash. I know God is real because I've seen with my own eyes how he works.

You may not feel God's hand on your shoulder or hear his voice in your ears. But you *can* see proof of the things God has done—and is still doing. It's just like seeing footprints in the sand—you might not see the person who made the footprints, but you can see the evidence that the person was there.

The Bible is like those footprints. It's all the proof you need to know that God is real. The Bible is full of real people—just like you—who tell their real stories about all the real things God has done in their lives. From eye-popping wonders like parting the sea to simple things like providing a meal, the Bible tells story after story about how much God loves us and craves our friendship.

You have a story, too, because God is at work in *your* life. And the more you read the Bible, the more you'll see God at work all around you every day.

—ELIJAH

Try It!

You can see proof of God in so many ways:

- In the good things other people do—Matthew 5:14-16
- Whenever you witness love, joy, peace, patience, kindness, goodness, faithfulness, gentleness, and self-control (the fruits of the Spirit)—Galatians 5:22-23
- In nature—Romans 1:19-20
- In all the things he gives you, like food and clothes—Philippians 4:19 and Matthew 6:31-33
- In the life of Jesus—Colossians 1:15
- In all the good things in your life—James 1:17

When have you seen God at work around you?
On a separate sheet of paper, write about it, or draw it.

Want more proof about how real God is?
Read these stories about times God showed himself to his people.

- God speaks through a burning bush—Exodus 3
- God sends a pillar of fire to protect the Israelites—Exodus 13:20-22
- God makes water flow out of a rock—Exodus 17:1-7

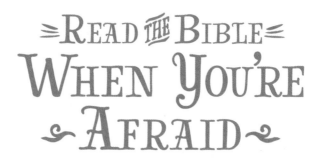

≈ READ THE BIBLE ≈
WHEN YOU'RE
⚘ AFRAID ⚘

"I prayed to the Lord, and he answered me.
He freed me from all my fears."

Psalm 34:4

I was *so* scared. My little brother was in danger. *Real* danger—the king wanted to kill every last Jewish baby boy. So my mom put my baby brother in a basket and set him in the reeds by the bank of a river. My tummy was in knots as I watched baby Moses from a distance! There was only one thing I could do about my fear: go to God.

There's one thing *you* can do when you're afraid, too: Go straight to God and his Word. The Bible tells tons of true stories about people in scary situations, even kids like me. When you read our stories, you'll learn what we learned: God is always with us.

What are you afraid of? When you read the Bible, you'll hear God tell you again and again not to be afraid. God is stronger than anything that scares you.

So what happened to my little brother? Was Moses okay? Did God save him? You can find out for yourself when you read our story in Exodus 2:1-10.

—MIRIAM

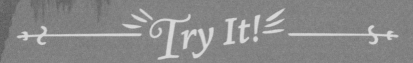

What's the scariest thing you've faced? How did God help you through it? Read what God has to say about fear in these Bible verses: Isaiah 41:10; Psalm 23:4; Psalm 56:3; 2 Timothy 1:7; and Philippians 4:6-7. Write out your favorite verse here.

Want to fight your fear?
Read these stories about how some of God's friends trusted God with their fears.

▸ Caleb knows God is bigger than his fears—Numbers 13

▸ Gideon learns to let go of his fears—Judges 6:1-32

▸ Jesus calms a storm—Mark 4:35-41

≈ READ THE BIBLE ≈
WHEN
YOU'RE SAD

*"Then Jesus said, 'Come to me, all of you
who are weary and carry heavy burdens,
and I will give you rest.'"*

Matthew 11:28

Can you imagine if the whole world didn't like you? If everyone ignored you, rejected you, and even hated you? That's exactly how God felt. He was so sad! People had turned their backs on him. And God's heart was broken.

But there was one person who still loved God: me. So when God decided to destroy the people on earth and start over, he spared me and my family. As the world drowned around me, I couldn't help wondering if the earth had been flooded with God's tears.

You've been sad, too, haven't you? Maybe a friend said something mean to you. Maybe your birthday party wasn't as fun as you'd hoped it would be. Maybe your pet died. So many things in life can bring us down. Everyone is sad sometimes.

But you're never alone in your sadness. God knows how you feel when your heart is broken. And you can always turn to God and his Word whenever your tears start to fall. God has so many good things to tell you in the Bible—things that will let you know that everything's going to be okay because God is with you.

—NOAH

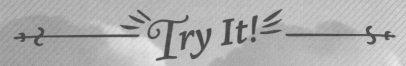
Read Noah's story in Genesis 6:9–9:1-17. Find some crayons or markers and draw the prettiest rainbow you can. Then place it somewhere to remind you that God will always comfort you when you're sad. Or you can draw your rainbow right here!

What should you read when you're feeling down?
Check out these stories about how God responds to our tears.

▸ David sings about God helping him through sadness—Psalm 40:1-5

▸ Paul talks about how much God loves us—Romans 8:31-39

▸ Jesus prays about his sadness—Mark 14:32-42

≋READ THE BIBLE≋
—WHEN—
YOU'RE ANGRY

"Human anger does not produce the righteousness God desires."

James 1:20

Uncontrolled anger is like a nasty disease. My husband, Nabal, was angry. All. The. Time. *Everything* made him mad, even when people were nice to him. Nabal was furious with David for asking for a little food after protecting our sheep...which made David angry, too. All of a sudden, they wanted to kill each other, and they would have, too, if I hadn't jumped in and stopped their rage with a little bit of kindness.

You know how it feels to be angry. Your body feels a little hotter, your face turns a little redder, and your muscles are a little tenser. Suddenly the world starts spinning, and you can't think about anything else. And you know that if you let your anger take over, you might hurt other people.

We all get angry sometimes, but God can help us overcome our anger. And I know the perfect thing to calm you down. It's the Bible! God filled the Bible with stories about how people dealt with anger. They either let it destroy them—like my husband—or they conquered anger with kindness—like me.

The Bible can help you relax and give you peace. God's words can remind you how much he loves you, and that's the happiest thing in the world!

—ABIGAIL

Try It!

Read Abigail's story about anger in 1 Samuel 25:2-38. Then think about a time when you got really, really mad. What happened? Did your anger make things worse? How did you stop being angry? Write what happened here.

Feeling mad?
See what happened when these Bible characters let their anger get the best of them.

▶ Cain gets mad at Abel—Genesis 4:1-16

▶ Joseph's brothers get mad at him—Genesis 37

▶ Moses gets mad at the Israelites—Exodus 32:15-35

READ THE BIBLE TO KNOW RIGHT FROM WRONG

"Let God transform you into a new person by changing the way you think. Then you will learn to know God's will for you, which is good and pleasing and perfect."

Romans 12:2

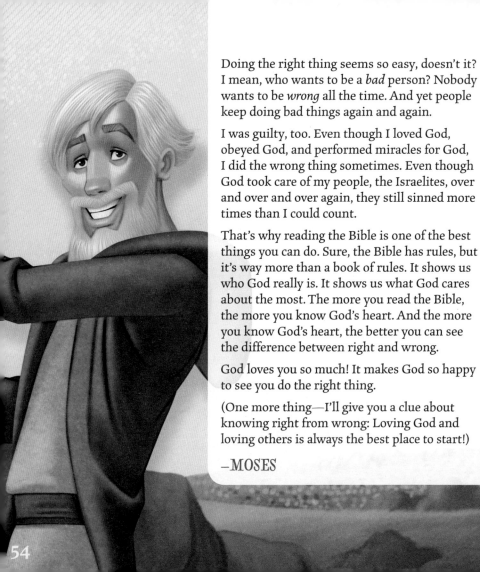

Doing the right thing seems so easy, doesn't it? I mean, who wants to be a *bad* person? Nobody wants to be *wrong* all the time. And yet people keep doing bad things again and again.

I was guilty, too. Even though I loved God, obeyed God, and performed miracles for God, I did the wrong thing sometimes. Even though God took care of my people, the Israelites, over and over and over again, they still sinned more times than I could count.

That's why reading the Bible is one of the best things you can do. Sure, the Bible has rules, but it's way more than a book of rules. It shows us who God really is. It shows us what God cares about the most. The more you read the Bible, the more you know God's heart. And the more you know God's heart, the better you can see the difference between right and wrong.

God loves you so much! It makes God so happy to see you do the right thing.

(One more thing—I'll give you a clue about knowing right from wrong: Loving God and loving others is always the best place to start!)

—MOSES

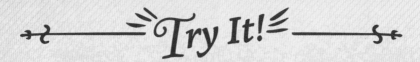

Try It!

Choose a friend or family member and read Exodus 20:1-17 together. It lists the Ten Commandments that God gave Moses. After you read them together, talk about how those rules show God's love for you. How would doing the things God has commanded us not to do hurt you and others? Write your answers here.

How can you tell right from wrong?
Read these Bible verses to see what God has to say about it.

▸ Adam and Eve make a bad choice—Genesis 3:1-19

▸ Jesus explains right and wrong—Mark 7:14-23

▸ Paul tells us how God helps us do the right thing—Romans 8:1-14

READ THE BIBLE TO DISCOVER WHY GOD MADE YOU

"For we are God's masterpiece. He has created us anew in Christ Jesus, so we can do the good things he planned for us long ago."

Ephesians 2:10

God made me beautiful. But he didn't make me good-looking so I could win beauty contests or become famous. God had a plan for me to save his people, and my pretty face made that possible.

See, the king of Persia wanted a new queen. He looked all over his kingdom for the prettiest woman he could find. And he picked me!

You might think being a queen is the ultimate dream. Sure, all the attention and the tasty food and the fancy clothes were nice. But life as a queen was scary, too. One of the king's assistants wanted to kill all my people—the Jews—and I had to risk my life to save them. I think *that's* why God made me pretty: so I could be the right person in the right place at the right time to do the right thing for my people.

It's not always easy to know exactly why God made you. God makes some people artists, other people teachers, some doctors, some helpers—he gives all kinds of great skills and talents. The Bible is the perfect place to read about how God created people with all sorts of gifts and purposes. It's exciting to explore what God might have in store for you!

But here's the most important thing to remember: God has one important purpose for *all* of us, and that's to love God and love other people. The Bible can show you how to do that! You'll see that you can be the right person in the right place at the right time to do the right thing, too.

—ESTHER

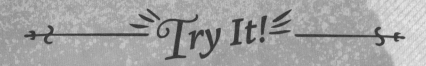

Try It!

Read about a man named Bezalel in Exodus 31:1-11. God gave Bezalel special skills and talents to make beautiful things that honored God. What's one beautiful thing you can make for God? Draw a picture of it here.

Want to read more about why God made you?
Explore God's purpose for some of the people in the Bible.

- Samuel tells the Israelites about God's purpose for them—1 Samuel 12:14-24
- Jeremiah tells the exiles about God's plans for them—Jeremiah 29:4-14
- Jesus tells us what's most important—Matthew 22:34-40

READ THE BIBLE WHEN YOU'RE FACING A BIG PROBLEM

"When troubles of any kind come your way, consider it an opportunity for great joy. For you know that when your faith is tested, your endurance has a chance to grow."

James 1:2-3

59

Five little rocks. That's all I had with me. No sword, no arrows, no helmet, no shield. Nothing but me, my sling, and five small stones. There I stood, alone in the middle of a battlefield, facing a giant warrior named Goliath. He was armed to the teeth, full of muscle and mayhem, gripping his giant spear. The glint in his steely eyes told me he couldn't wait to chew me up and spit me out.

It was a *big* problem, no doubt about it.

But I knew something the giant didn't know: It wasn't the rocks that would win the battle for me. It was something bigger. Way bigger than me, bigger than the giant, and bigger than the huge army standing behind him. It was God. With God on my side, there was no way I could lose.

You can be a hero, too! God can give you the strength and courage to stand up to all the problems in your life, even the *big* ones. The more you read your Bible, the more ready you'll be to face your own giants. And with God on your side, you can do the most heroic thing of all: share God's love with everyone you know.

—DAVID

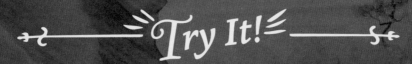

Try It!

Read the thrilling story of David and Goliath in 1 Samuel 17:1-51.
Draw a picture of small David standing next to giant Goliath,
then draw a picture of you facing a big problem in your life.

No problem is too big or too small for God.
Read these Bible stories about how God helped his friends with their problems.

▶ God helps Job with his terrible troubles—Job 1; 2; 13:20-28; 40; and 42

▶ God helps Joseph through *lots* of problems—Genesis 37; 39–47

▶ God talks to Paul about Paul's big problem—2 Corinthians 12:7-10

READ THE BIBLE TO DISCOVER GOD'S PROMISES

"And because of his glory and excellence, he has given us great and precious promises. These are the promises that enable you to share his divine nature and escape the world's corruption caused by human desires."

2 Peter 1:4

Say it with me: "Old ladies don't have babies!"

So when God told me I was going to be a mama, I just had to laugh. I was an old lady! And as we all know, "Old ladies don't have babies!" But God had the last laugh. God kept his promise, and I gave birth to my first son when I was 90 years old.

Ninety years old! I have wrinkles, for goodness' sake!

But God had made a promise to give me and Abraham a huge family. And when God makes a promise, he *always* keeps it. God does things in his own way—the way that only God can do them.

You don't have to take my word for it. You can read about *thousands* of promises God made—and kept—in the Bible. Story after story after story shows you how much God loves you, and that's a promise you can count on forever.

—SARAH

63

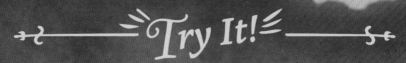

Try It!

Read Genesis 18:1-15 and 21:1-7, the story about God's promise to give Sarah a baby. Why do you think Sarah laughed? (She even named her baby Isaac, which means *laughter*.) What's something funny that's happened to you? Write about it below.

Wonder what kinds of promises God has for you?
Read these Bible verses to discover a few.

- ▸ God promises to make you strong—Isaiah 40:29-31
- ▸ God promises to give you what you need—Philippians 4:19
- ▸ God promises to never stop loving you—Psalm 136:26

READ THE BIBLE TO LEARN HOW TO MAKE FRIENDS

"So now we can rejoice in our wonderful new relationship with God because our Lord Jesus Christ has made us friends of God."

Romans 5:11

We had lost everything. Our husbands had died. We had no money, no home, no food, and no future. Things were looking hopeless for the two of us.

There was only one thing that kept us going: friendship. We had God, and we had each other. And that turned out to be more than enough.

Friends are one of life's greatest gifts. They're the people who play with us, laugh with us, and stick with us through the good and bad times. We got through the hardest times in our life because of our friendships...with each other and with God.

The Bible is full of stories of great companions—David and Jonathan, Jesus and his disciples, and the two of us. You can learn a lot about true friendship when you read our stories in the Bible. You could even say the Bible is the ultimate handbook on friendship, especially about how to be friends with God himself!

—RUTH AND NAOMI

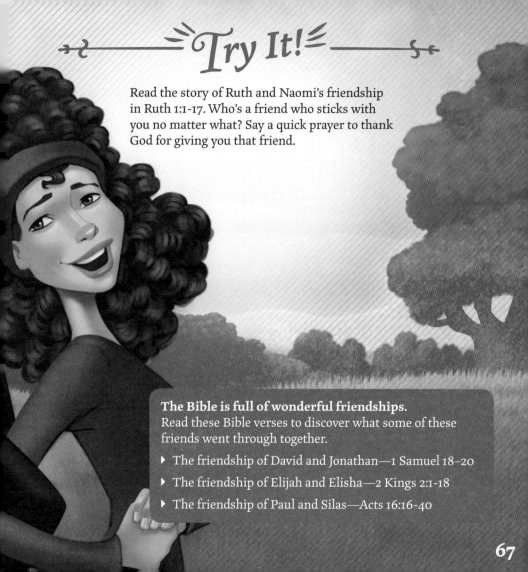

Try It!

Read the story of Ruth and Naomi's friendship in Ruth 1:1-17. Who's a friend who sticks with you no matter what? Say a quick prayer to thank God for giving you that friend.

The Bible is full of wonderful friendships.
Read these Bible verses to discover what some of these friends went through together.

▸ The friendship of David and Jonathan—1 Samuel 18–20

▸ The friendship of Elijah and Elisha—2 Kings 2:1-18

▸ The friendship of Paul and Silas—Acts 16:16-40

READ THE BIBLE
WHEN YOU'RE NOT GETTING ALONG WITH SOMEONE

"Do all that you can to live in peace with everyone."

Romans 12:18

Hot and cold. Night and day. Bitter and sweet. That was my brother Esau and me—pretty much opposites. Even though we were twins, we couldn't have been more different. And we did *not* get along. At all.

It was more or less all my fault. I cheated Esau out of his inheritance, and then I lied and tricked our dad into giving his blessing to me instead of my brother. I was selfish. My brother was so mad I thought he was going to kill me!

Fighting with someone is one of the worst feelings in the world. You feel sick because your blood is boiling, your stomach's in knots, and your heart feels like it's going to explode.

How do you know what to do when someone is really mad at you?

The Bible is the best place to go when you have problems with other people. God shows you what happens when people love and forgive each other instead of squabbling, scuffling, and struggling.

When you look to God and the Bible to discover how to get along with each other, life just gets better. I should know; when my brother hugged me and forgave me, it was the best feeling of my entire life.

—JACOB

Try It!

Think about a friend or sibling you've had some trouble with. Read these proverbs about friendship: Proverbs 16:28; 17:9; 19:22; 27:17; and 28:13. What can you learn about getting along with others from those proverbs?

People had a lot of fights and arguments in the Bible. But thanks to God's grace, they often made up.
Here are a few of those stories you can read.

▸ Joseph forgives his brothers—Genesis 45

▸ King David is kind to his enemy's family—2 Samuel 9

▸ The prodigal son returns home—Luke 15:11-24

READ THE BIBLE TO BECOME WISER

"If you need wisdom, ask our generous God, and he will give it to you."

James 1:5

If you could have anything in the world—
anything—what would you ask for? Piles of
money? Super powers? Popularity? To play
and have fun every day? Maybe the world's
largest doughnut?

When God told me I could ask for
anything, there was one thing I wanted
more than anything else: wisdom. That
made God very happy. In fact, God granted
my wish. God gave me wisdom...and so
much more.

Wisdom is more than just knowing
something. Wisdom is seeing the world
through God's eyes. It's understanding
how God thinks about stuff.

And here's the coolest part: If you ask God
for wisdom, he'll give it to you, too!

Can kids be wise? Yes! And you can
become wiser the more you read the Bible.
The Bible is *full* of wisdom. Just about
every page can help you see the world as
God sees it. You can't ask for a better super
power than that.

—SOLOMON

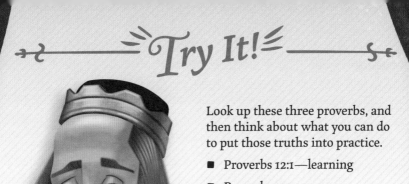

Try It!

Look up these three proverbs, and then think about what you can do to put those truths into practice.

- Proverbs 12:1—learning
- Proverbs 15:1—anger
- Proverbs 31:9—helping others

Solomon wasn't the only wise person in the Bible. Read about these other people who tapped into God's wisdom.

- ▸ Deborah makes wise decisions—Judges 4
- ▸ Bezalel uses God's wisdom to create art—Exodus 31:1-11
- ▸ Stephen speaks with wisdom in the synagogue—Acts 6:8-15

≋READ THE BIBLE≋
═TO HELP═
YOU PRAY

"Don't worry about anything; instead, pray about everything. Tell God what you need, and thank him for all he has done."

Philippians 4:6

All I wanted was a baby. Every night I dreamed of holding my child in my arms and singing him lullabies until he fell asleep. Every day I imagined playing with my son and hearing him laugh. But year after year went by, and I still didn't have a baby.

I prayed and prayed and prayed and prayed and prayed. I begged God to give me my own little boy. I went to the Tabernacle and cried and prayed some more. I even told God that if he gave me a son, I would give my child back to God.

God finally answered my prayer. It may have taken longer than I'd hoped, but God heard me.

Sometimes we're not sure what to pray about or how to pray. Talking with God might seem hard. But when you read the Bible, you can find lots of examples of people talking with God. The Bible can guide you to learn how to pray, why to pray, and what to pray for.

—HANNAH

Try It!

Look up these three psalms and read them aloud as prayers to God.

- Psalm 42:5
- Psalm 139:14-18
- Psalm 145:15-16

So many Bible stories include prayers. Read these stories about how prayer made a big difference.

▶ King Hezekiah prays for Jerusalem's protection—2 Kings 19:10-19, 35-36

▶ Daniel prays to interpret a dream—Daniel 2:1-19

▶ The church prays for Peter in prison —Acts 12:1-11

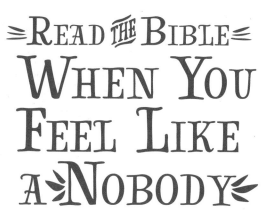

≋Read the Bible≋
When You Feel Like a Nobody

"How precious are your thoughts about me, O God. They cannot be numbered! I can't even count them; they outnumber the grains of sand!"

Psalm 139:17-18

If you made a list of the most important people in the world, we definitely wouldn't be on it. We just watched stinky, boring sheep every day. No one cared much about us.

But God cared. He loved us even though we were just a bunch of nobodies. In fact, God valued us so much that we were the first people he told about the birth of Jesus, his Son. God sent a giant group of angels to tell *us* the news. We even got to see baby Jesus in the manger!

Don't forget! In God's eyes there's no such thing as a nobody. The Bible makes that clear, with story after story of ordinary people God loved and thought of as *very* important.

Anytime you think you don't matter, read the Bible to see how much God values *everyone*— including you. God has promises and special plans just for *you*. Of all the people who've ever lived, God has chosen *you* to do something special. (Read Galatians 5:22-23 for the details.)

–THE SHEPHERDS

Read the story of another person in the Bible who thought he wasn't very important—but God did. You can find Gideon's suspenseful story in Judges 6–8. When you depend on God, anything is possible!

God liked choosing the "nobodies" of the world to accomplish many of his greatest tasks. Dig into a few of those stories by reading these Bible verses.

▸ Jesus chooses fishermen to be his disciples —Matthew 4:18-22

▸ God selects a young shepherd to be a king —1 Samuel 16:1-14

▸ Jesus asks a short, hated swindler to be his friend—Luke 19:1-10

READ THE BIBLE WHEN YOU HAVE QUESTIONS OR DOUBTS

*"For the word of the Lord holds true,
and we can trust everything he does."*

Psalm 33:4

When my friends told me Jesus was alive, I didn't believe them. After all, I'd seen Jesus die with my own eyes. I watched them bury his body in a tomb. Jesus, my best friend who I loved so much, was gone. He was dead.

How could Jesus come back to life? It was too good to be true. So I had my doubts. Lots of them.

But when Jesus showed up one night—as alive as alive could be—he walked right up to me and showed me his hands. He let me touch his wounds and see for myself that it was really him. Jesus was alive!

Jesus didn't mind my doubts. He was happy to show me the proof I needed when I wasn't sure I believed.

Lots of people find things in the Bible they don't understand. It's okay to be confused. God welcomes our doubts and questions. Sometimes you might read something in the Bible that doesn't make sense to you, and that's all right. Keep reading and keep praying. God will help you understand.

—THOMAS

One great way to spend time with the Bible is to meditate on it. *Meditate* means to think hard about something, usually in a quiet place without distractions. Read what God has to say about meditation in Psalm 1:2; Joshua 1:8; and Philippians 4:8.

Thomas isn't the only Bible character who asked big questions.
Read some of the Bible's other big questions—and answers—in these verses.

▸ David asks, "How can a young person stay pure?"—Psalm 119:9-10

▸ Nicodemus asks, "How can I be born again when I'm old?"—John 3:1-21

▸ Jesus asks, "Who do you say that I am?"—Matthew 16:13-17

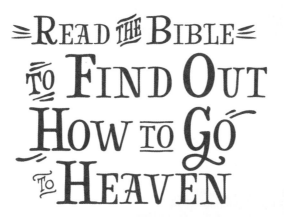

READ THE BIBLE TO FIND OUT HOW TO GO TO HEAVEN

"I tell you the truth, those who listen to my message and believe in God who sent me have eternal life."

John 5:24

83

Stop for a minute and imagine the most beautiful place you can think of. A place with the greenest trees and the bluest skies. The streets and buildings are made of gleaming, sparkling gold.

But that's not all.

Imagine a smile on the face of everyone you meet. No one cries; no one gets mad; no one says mean things. You never feel pain, and you and all your friends will never die. Angels will be your neighbors, and Jesus will be your King. Think about the happiest you've ever felt in your life...and then multiply it by a million.

That's heaven, my friend. It's a place God is preparing for you and everyone else who believes in Jesus.

The Bible tells you exactly how to get to heaven after you die. Jesus talked about heaven a lot, because he wants everyone to live with him there forever. And when you believe in Jesus, I will see you there someday!

—JOHN

Try It!

Read the following verses that tell us what God says about being with him forever in heaven: John 3:16-18; Romans 6:23 and 10:9; Ephesians 2:8-9; and 1 John 4:10 and 5:12. Then tonight before you go to sleep, thank God for sending Jesus so that you, too, can be with him in heaven someday.

What will heaven be like?
The Bible doesn't give us many details, but God does give us a few clues in these verses.

▸ Jesus is in heaven right now—Acts 1:1-11

▸ Christians go to heaven when they die—Philippians 1:21-23

▸ John describes his vision of heaven—Revelation 21:3-4

READ THE BIBLE TO DISCOVER WHY JESUS LOVES YOU SO MUCH!

"For this is how God loved the world: He gave his one and only Son, so that everyone who believes in him will not perish but have eternal life."

John 3:16

Who in your life do you love a lot? Your mom? Your dad? Your grandparents? Your pet? Your best friend?

I love you even more than that. *Way* more. When I think about you, I smile! (And I think about you all the time!) And I'm always with you. *Always.* Even though you can't see me or hear my voice, I'm always nearby. I'm just a prayer away.

The Bible is all about me and how much I love you. I want you to read your Bible to discover more about my heart, to spend time with me, and to learn what it means to follow me. The more you discover about me in the Bible, the more you'll become like me.

Most of all, I want to be your best friend. When you read your Bible, imagine me sitting next to you. Picture me telling you those stories, as if I were with you face to face. Because the Bible is my story...and it's *your* story, too!

—JESUS

Try It!

Read Matthew 14:23-33, the story about the time Jesus walked on water. Isn't Jesus amazing? Draw a picture of you walking with Jesus on the water, and place it somewhere to remind you to put your faith in Jesus every day.

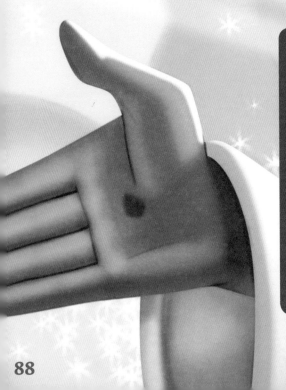

Jesus is *amazing*!
You can find so many wonderful things about Jesus in the Bible. Here are a few more stories you don't want to miss.

▸ Jesus feeds 5,000 people with a boy's lunch—Matthew 14:13-21

▸ Jesus tells stories about God's kingdom—Mark 4:1-34

▸ Jesus visits Mary and Martha—Luke 10:38-42

▸ Jesus washes his followers' feet—John 13:1-17

▸ Jesus rises from the dead —John 20:1-18

WHERE TO TURN IN THE BIBLE WHEN...

The Bible can help you with just about anything! Whenever you have questions or problems, God has answers ready for you in the Bible. Read God's words and let him help you.

WHEN I FEEL ANGRY

Psalm 37:8
Proverbs 15:1; 19:11
Luke 6:27-31
John 13:34-35
Ephesians 4:26-27, 31-32
Colossians 3:8-10

WHEN I FEEL AFRAID

Psalm 46:10; 56:3; 91:11; 118:6
Isaiah 41:10
Ephesians 6:11-12
James 1:2-3

WHEN I FEEL ALONE

Joshua 1:9
Psalm 139:1-6
Isaiah 41:10
Matthew 28:20
Philippians 4:13

WHEN I FEEL ASHAMED

Luke 15:10
John 1:12; 3:17-18
2 Corinthians 5:17
1 John 1:9

When I Feel Sad

Psalm 34:19
John 14:27; 16:33
Philippians 4:6-7
James 1:2-4

When I Feel Jealous

Proverbs 14:30; 23:17-18
Matthew 6:19-21
1 Corinthians 13:4-5
James 3:14-16

When I Feel Tempted

Matthew 26:41
1 Corinthians 10:13
Galatians 6:1
Ephesians 6:11-12
Hebrews 2:18

When I Feel Worried

Psalm 46:10
Isaiah 40:31
Matthew 6:25-26, 33-34; 11:28
Romans 8:28
Philippians 4:6-7
1 Peter 5:7

When I Need Confidence

Psalm 139:14
Matthew 5:16
John 15:5
2 Corinthians 5:17
Ephesians 6:11-12
Philippians 4:13
Hebrews 4:16

When I Need Encouragement

Matthew 6:33-34; 11:28
Luke 11:9
John 1:12
Romans 8:28
Philippians 4:6-7, 13
1 Thessalonians 5:11

When I Need Forgiveness

2 Chronicles 7:14
Nehemiah 9:17
Luke 6:9-11, 31; 15:10
John 3:17-18
Colossians 3:13
1 John 1:9

When I Need to Forgive Someone

Luke 6:27-31
1 Corinthians 13:4-10
Ephesians 4:32
Colossians 3:13

When I Need Help

Psalm 23; 121:1-2
Isaiah 40:31; 41:10
Luke 11:9
John 15:5
Ephesians 6:11-12
Revelation 3:20

When I Need to Obey

Deuteronomy 6:5-6
Mark 16:15
John 13:34; 14:15
Romans 12:1-2, 13

When I Need Patience

Psalm 37:7; 46:10
Matthew 6:33-34
Galatians 5:22

When I Need Wisdom

Proverbs 1:7; 10:14
Jeremiah 33:3
Matthew 6:19-21
John 14:26
Ephesians 6:11-12
James 1:5

When I Have Doubts About God

Psalm 19:1; 46:10
Luke 21:33
John 1:1, 14; 3:16; 14:6; 20:31
Hebrews 4:16; 11:1
1 John 4:10

When I Don't Know

What Decision to Make

Deuteronomy 6:5-6
Matthew 19:19
Luke 6:31
John 14:26
Romans 12:1-2
Galatians 6:7
James 1:6

When I Don't Know How to Pray

Psalm 100:4; 118:1
Luke 6:27-30; 11:9
1 Thessalonians 5:16-18
Matthew 6:5-13

When I'm Worried That I might Not Go to Heaven

John 3:16-18
Romans 6:23; 10:9
Ephesians 2:8-9
1 John 4:10; 5:12

When My Friends Talk About Me Behind My Back

Luke 6:31
Romans 3:23
Ephesians 4:32
Philippians 4:6-7
Colossians 3:13
1 Peter 3:9

When I'm Afraid to Tell Others About Jesus

Isaiah 55:10-11
Matthew 5:15-16; 28:19-20
Acts 1:8
Romans 1:16
2 Corinthians 2:14-17
Hebrews 11:6
1 Peter 3:15
1 John 3:18

When My Parents Fight

Psalm 23; 46:1
Matthew 6:33-34; 11:28
Philippians 4:6-7
Hebrews 4:16

YOU'LL ALSO LOVE...

FREE Bible App

Experience the Bible in a more personal way with the free *Friends With God* app.

Friends With God Story Bible

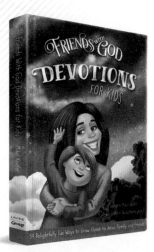

*Friends With God
Devotions for Kids*

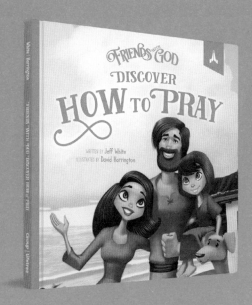

*Friends With God
Discover How to Pray*

*Friends With God
Sing-Along Songs*

Group | **lifetree**

Visit your favorite Christian resource provider for more Friends With God resources!

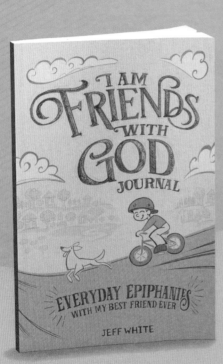

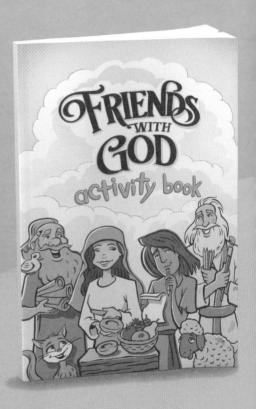

*I Am Friends With
God Journal*

*Friends With God
Activity Book*